Celebrate

Islamic Festivals

Series editor: Jan Thompson

Khadijah Knight

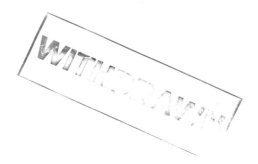

First published in Great Britain by
Heinemann Publishers (Oxford) Ltd
Halley Court, Jordan Hill, Oxford OX2 8EJ

MADRID ATHENS PARIS FLORENCE PRAGUE
WARSAW PORTSMOUTH NH CHICAGO
SAO PAULO SINGAPORE TOKYO MELBOURNE
AUCKLAND IBADAN GABORONE
JOHANNESBURG

Designed by Sue Clarke
Illustrated by Jeff Edwards
Colour reproduction by Track QSP

Printed in Hong Kong / China

03 02 01
10 9 8 7 6 5

ISBN 0 431 06955 7

This title is also available in a hardback library edition
(ISBN 0 431 06951 4)

British Library Cataloguing in Publication Data
Knight, Khadijah
    Islamic Festivals. - (Celebrate Series)
    I. Title II. Series
    297.36

Acknowledgements
The author would like to thank the following people for
helping with this book by having their pictures taken or by
giving their views on the writing:

Hussain Khan and his family; Fatime Meyzin and her family;
Ibrahim Muhammad and his family; Muhsin J Kilby and his
family; members of the most honourable Naqshbandi Sufi
order; Islamic Consultancy and Information Services, PO
Box 2842, London W6 9ZH; Islamic Consultancy and
Information Services of Scotland, 127 Cumbernauld Road,
Stepps, Glasgow G33 6EY.

The Publishers would like to thank the following for
permission to reproduce photographs.

Muhsin Jak Kilby: p.4, p.5; C S Nielsen/Bruce Coleman
Limited: p.6; Muhsin Jak Kilby: p.8, p.9, p.10; Trip: p.11; Muhsin
Jak Kilby: p.12, p.13, p.14, p.15, p.16; Sayyed Jaffer al-Bassam:
p.17; R Dalmaine/Barnaby's Picture Library: p.18; Gobet-APF:
p.19; Muhsin Jak Kilby: p.20, p.21, p.22, p.24, p.25, p.26, p.27,
p.28, p.29; Peter Sanders: p.30; Trip/A Di Nola: p.31; Muhsin
Jak Kilby: p.32; Circa Photo Library: p.33; Muhsin Jak Kilby:
p.34; Muslim Aid, Islamic Relief, Human Appeal International:
p.35; Muhsin Jak Kilby: p.36, p.38; Trip: p. 39; Muhsin Jak Kilby:
p.40, p.41, p.42, p.43

Cover photograph is reproduced with the permission of
Peter Sanders.

Our thanks to Denise Cush of Bath College of Higher
Education and to Elizabeth Bladon for their comments in
the preparation of this book.

Every effort has been made to contact copyright holders of
any material reproduced in this book. Any omissions will be
rectified in subsequent printings if notice is given to the
Publisher.

**Whenever Muslims mention the Prophet
Muhammad, the words 'peace and blessings of
Allah upon him' are said in Arabic. This is shown
in this book in the abbreviated form of 'PBUH'.
Whenever prophets and the twelve Shi'ah
Imams are mentioned, Muslims say 'peace be
upon him'. This is shown in this book in the
abbreviated form of 'PUH'.**

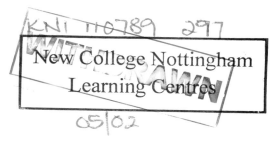

Contents

Introduction   4

Festivals   6

The Qur'an   8
The final book of guidance

Hadith   10
The sayings of the
Prophet Muhammad PBUH

Salah   12
Communicating with
and worshipping Allah

Hijrah   14
The Prophet Muhammad's
migration to Madinah

Ahlul-Bayt   16
The people of the house
of the Prophet PBUH

Ashura   18
The martyrdom of
Husain ibn Ali PUH

Maulid   20
The birthday of the
Prophet Muhammad PBUH

Laylat-ul-Isra
wal Mi'raj   22
The night journey
and ascension

Laylat-ul-Barat   24
The night of forgiveness

Ramadan:
the ninth month (1)   26
Fasting with the family

Ramadan:
the ninth month (2)   28
Fasting with the community

Laylat-ul-Qadr   30
The night of power

Id-ul-Fitr   32
The festival of breaking the fast

Sadaqah, zakah, khums   34
Giving for the sake of Allah

Hajj   36
The pilgrimage

A Hajj diary   38
Diary of the pilgrimage

Id-ul-Adha   40
Festival of the sacrifice

Jumu'ah   42
The weekly Friday
congregational prayer

Glossary   44

Further reading   46

A closer look   47

Index   48

Introduction

This unit tells you who Muslims are and what they believe.

Husain and Fatimah are both **Muslims**. Husain is 11 and Fatimah is 8. Fatimah has two older brothers, Mehmet and Mahmoud. Their family works hard to help Muslims in Britain keep their Islamic traditions.

Who is a Muslim?

Anyone, anywhere, whatever their race or nationality, can be or become a Muslim at any time during their life. A Muslim is someone who believes that there is only one God – **Allah**, the Creator of everything. Muslims believe that Allah sent messengers and books to teach people to live a good life. Muslims try to be at peace with themselves and with all of Allah's creatures and creation by following the principles of Islam. They believe that these were revealed to Allah's final messenger, the Prophet Muhammad PBUH. They are only part of what makes a person a good Muslim.

Every Friday Husain, his parents and his sister Maryam go to the mosque, where everyone recites the Qur'an and Allah's beautiful names.

What is Islam?

Islam is the way people live following Allah's guidance. Islam is 'the natural way of life' for more than a thousand million people in the world today. Islam teaches that everything that people do is written down by angels and will be judged by Allah on the Day of Judgement. Allah will decide how people will be rewarded for their good deeds and punished for their bad actions. Muslims believe that Allah is just and merciful.

The two main branches of Islam are **Sunni** and **Shi'ah**. All Muslims follow the teachings of the **Qur'an** – Allah's revealed book and the example of the Prophet Muhammad PBUH.

The principles of Islam

Shahadah – *the statement of belief that 'There is no god except Allah and Muhammad is the Messenger of Allah'.*

Salah – *worship of Allah. Muslims have to recite salah five times a day in Arabic.*

Sawm – *fasting during daylight hours in the month of Ramadan.*

Zakah – *making payment of 2.5 per cent welfare tax on wealth.*

Hajj – *going on pilgrimage.*

Fatimah wears a headscarf not only for salah but all the time. Husain keeps his head covered too, either with a hat or a turban.

Festivals

This unit explains how Muslims organize their year.

By watching for the new moon and by observing each of its phases, Muslims have a calendar in the sky.

Moon phases

All **Muslims** use a lunar calendar. It is called the **Hijrah** calendar, and began when the Prophet Muhammad PBUH moved to **Madinah**. The word Hijrah means 'emigration' or 'departure'. Each month starts by seeing the new moon. There are 12 months in the Islamic calendar. The Islamic lunar year is about 11 days shorter than the 365-day fixed calendar. Each year, each Islamic month starts 11 days earlier than the year before. There are no fixed winter, spring or harvest festivals in Islam.

'It is not permitted to the sun to catch up the moon, nor can the night outstrip the day: each just swims along in its own orbit according to the law.' (**Qur'an** 36:40.)

'The number of months in the sight of **Allah** is 12 in a year – so ordained by Him the day He created the heavens and the earth.' (Qur'an 9:36.)

The sun

The sun has a useful part to play in understanding the Muslim day. For Muslims, each day ends and another begins at sunset. When the sun sets on Thursday, Friday begins. Even if there were no clocks, Muslims could work out the time to offer **salah** five times a day from the position of the sun in the sky. They start very early with the **fajr**, the dawn salah, before the sun has come up.

Times to offer Salah

Salat-ul-Fajr is between the first light of dawn and sunrise.
Salat-ul-Zuhr is after midday.
Salat-ul-Asr is the mid-afternoon.
Salat-ul-Maghrib is sunset.
Salat-ul-Isha is from an hour and a half after sunset.

This Islamic calendar wheel shows some Islamic events in the lunar year, which begins with the month of Muharram.

12 Dhul-Hijjah

8–10 The Hajj
Commemorates events in the life of the Prophets Ibrahim, Ismail and Muhammad (peace and blessings upon them all)
10–12 Id ul-Adah
The feast of Sacrifice which is part of the Hajj

1 Muharram

1 Hijrah-Emigration
Prophet PBUH moves Madinah 622CE. calender counted this date

10 Ashura
The death of the Prophet's Imam Hussein PUH at Kerbala in Iraq 680 CE

2 Safar

3 Rabi' al-Awwal
12–17 Maulid an-Nabi
Celebrates the birth, life and example of Muhammad PBUH

11 Dhul-Qad'ah

4 Rabi' al-Thani

10 Shawal
1 Id ul-Fitr
Festival to mark the start of the new year and the end of fasting

9 Ramadan
The fasting month
Ordered by Allah in the Qur'an
23–27 Laylat ul-Qadr
The night of power on which the Qur'an was first revealed

5 Jumada al-Awwal

20 The Birthday of Fatimah Zarah
The daughter of the Prophet Muhammad PBUH and mother of Imam Hussain PUH is called the leader of women

6 Jumada al-Thani

27 Laylat ul-Isra wal Mi'raj
The night journey and ascent of the Prophet Muhammad PBUH Makkah to Jerusalem and through the heavens

7 Rajab

14–15 Laylat ul-Barat
The night when Allah decides what will happen in the coming year, to all His creation

8 Sha'ban

The Qur'an

This unit tells you about the final book of guidance.

Muslims believe that the **Qur'an** is **Allah**'s final book of guidance, which was revealed to the Prophet Muhammad PBUH for all humankind.

Fatimah is studying her Arabic reading book to learn the words that are written in the Qu'ran.

The language of the Qur'an

The language of the Qur'an is Arabic. No matter where they live or what their language is, **Muslims** always read or recite the Qur'an in Arabic. The words themselves have a special sound. Although it is a very long book, millions of people know it by heart. The Qur'an has 114 **surahs**, or sections. Each surah is made up of shorter numbered sections. These are the numbers which follow the Qur'an quotes in this book. The Qur'an can also be read in 30 portions, one a day for a month, or in seven portions, one for each day of the week. Muslims often read and study translations of the Qur'an in their own language.

66 **I am learning to read the Qur'an. First we have to learn the Arabic alphabet. Then we work out how the words sound. Sometimes they sound like a tune. That makes it easier to learn.** 99
– Fatimah

Zayd ibn Thabit

In **Madinah**, 12-year-old Zayd ibn Thabit offered to
fight to defend the Muslim community. The Prophet
PBUH was pleased that Zayd was so brave, but said
that he was too young to fight. Zayd thought of
another way he could help. He could read and write
very well, and worked hard at learning to recite the
Qur'an. The Prophet PBUH asked him to learn
Hebrew, so that he could write letters to the local
Jewish tribes. Later, he learned to read, write and
speak the Syriac language. He often wrote down
parts of the Qur'an soon after they were revealed to
the Prophet PBUH. When the Prophet PBUH died,
Zayd was given the job of collecting all the
parchments and palm leaves on which the Qur'an
had been written. With the help of assistants he
organized and made copies of everything exactly as
it was taught by the Prophet PBUH.

'When the Qur'an is read, listen to it with attention
in silence that you may receive [Allah's] mercy'.
(Qur'an 7:204.)

After school or
at weekends,
lots of Muslim
children go to
classes to
learn what the
Qu'ran
teaches.

Hadith

This unit tells you about the sayings of the Prophet Muhammad PBUH.

Even though she listens very carefully, unless Fatimah writes down telephone messages, she sometimes gets them mixed up.

❝ Sometimes, our teacher lets us play 'Chinese Whispers'. He whispers a message into one child's ear. Then it is passed one by one around the class. It nearly always comes out wrong. My dad says I'm like that with telephone messages. ❞
– *Fatimah*

The hadith
The word '**hadith**' means 'saying'. The hadith are reports of what the Prophet Muhammad PBUH said. Because he was the living example of Islamic teaching, what Muhammad PBUH said about how to live is very important to **Muslims**. People who were close to him remembered what he had said and told it to others. Some wrote it down. After the Prophet Muhammad PBUH passed away, people realized it was necessary to collect all the reports of what he had said. That way, the knowledge could be spread widely. The hadith became the second source of all Islamic teaching after the **Qur'an**. Islamic law is based upon the Qur'an and people learn about the customs of the Prophet PBUH through the hadith.

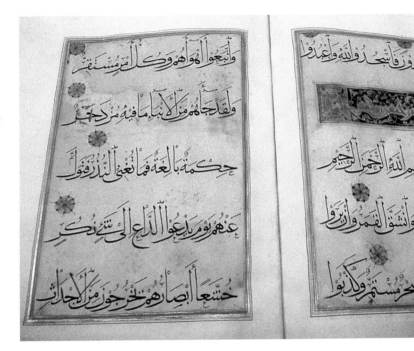

These are pages of the Qu'ran – Allah's words. The hadith are reports of what the Prophet Muhammad P.BUH said and did.

How the hadith were collected and checked

Every hadith which was reported was checked. The person who had told it had to be known to be truthful. What they said had to match what was known about the Prophet PBUH and Islamic teaching. Because it had to be reliable, collecting hadith was very careful work. If there was any doubt about a hadith being correct, it was not added to the collections. Many scholars spent their lives doing this work. Some of the most famous collections are:

Sahih al-Bukhari – the collection compiled by Muhammad al-Bukhari

Sahih Muslim – the books of hadith gathered by Abul Husayn Muslim

al-Kafi – those collected by Muhammad ibn Yaqub Koleini

Beautiful Hadith

Abdullah ibn Amr reported:
The dearest of you to me is the one who is best in conduct.
(Hadith: Bukhari.)

Ja'bar reported:
Every good deed is a charity, and it is a good deed to meet people with a cheerful face.
(Hadith: Tirmidhi.)

Oqbah ibn A'mer reported:
... All of you are the children of Adam ... There is no superiority of anyone over another except in faith.
(Hadith: Bayhaqi.)

Salah

This unit tells you how Muslims communicate with and worship Allah.

" **When I was really little, I used to try to do salah. My mum says I used to copy her. When she bowed down, I would lie on the prayer mat in front of her. As I got a bit older, she would tell me to stand beside her and show me what to do. My granny and grandpa helped me learn the Arabic words of the salah.** "
– *Fatimah*

The meanings of prayer positions
Performing **salah** is not only saying particular words but also making specific movements. Someone even called salah 'the Yoga of Islam' because the physical positions help **Muslims** to think about what they are doing and saying to **Allah**. When Muslims pray they take positions which remind them of how they should behave in front of their Creator.

The obligation to pray
When Muslim children are 7 years old, their parents must ask them to perform salah. As they reach puberty, it is up to the young people to make sure they do all their five times salah every day. As Allah says in the **Qur'an**: '...And establish regular prayers at the two ends of the day, and at the approaches of the night: for those things that are good remove those that are evil...' (Qur'an 11:114).

While they offer salah, the children turn towards the Ka'bah in Makkah.

Salah positions

Stand upright: *be upright and well-behaved.*

Bow low: *show respect and reverence.*

Kneel down: *show thankfulness.*

Prostrate: *show readiness to do what Allah wants.*

Prayer mats

Some Muslims have a favourite mat they use to pray on at home. Mats can be made from straw or cotton or be a woollen carpet. They often have an arch shape at the top end. When someone is going to use the mat for salah, they lay it in the direction of **Makkah**. **Shi'ah** Muslims often put a small tablet of clay from Kerbala on the place where their forehead touches the mat (see pages 18–19).

Hijrah

This unit describes the Prophet Muhammad's migration to Madinah.

On the **Hijrah**, in **Muslim** communities and schools where some of the pupils are Muslims, the story of the Prophet's move to **Madinah** on the first day of **Muharram** is told.

> " **Our calendar starts from the day that the Prophet Muhammad PBUH arrived in Madinah to live. My friends think it's funny that our New Year doesn't often start on 1 January. But I've worked out that in the year 2008 CE, the Islamic year of 1430 will start at the beginning of January, too. I'll be grown up then.**
> – *Fatimah* "

Leaving Makkah

In the year 622 CE the Prophet Muhammad's life was threatened. He had been teaching people in **Makkah** about **Allah** and that it was wrong to worship idols and to be greedy and cruel. Many of the people of Makkah were making money from idol-worship and they didn't want to lose their business. They tried to bribe Muhammad PBUH to stop him speaking out, but he would not accept their money.

From the map of Arabia, Fatimah can see how far it is from Makkah to Madinah.

A Muslim song

Muslims sing 'Tala'al badru alaynaa', the song the women and children of Madinah sang to welcome the Prophet PBUH to the safety of their town. Some verses from Tala'al badru alaynaa in English are:

The full moon has arisen
 among us,
We must be thankful
Whenever a messenger calls
 us to Allah.
Oh Messenger, you have come
 with
A call which must be obeyed.
You have come and honoured
 Madinah.
Welcome, oh the best of men.

One night he heard that they planned to kill him. His cousin Ali PUH spent that night in the Prophet's house so that it didn't look empty. Meanwhile, Muhammad PBUH and his friend Abu Bakr escaped into the desert. The plotters were furious when they found that he had got away. For a few days the Prophet PBUH and Abu Bakr hid. Then they criss-crossed the desert, all the way north to Madinah. The people of Madinah were really glad that he was coming to live with them. They knew he was a wise and good leader and would help their community.

To show their love for the Prophet PBUH, Muslims visit his mosque in Madinah.

Ahlul-Bayt

This unit is about the people of the house of the Prophet PBUH.

Who are the family of the Prophet PBUH?

The Prophet Muhammad PBUH and his wife Khadijah had sons who sadly died while they were still infants. Happily, their beloved daughter Fatimah Zahrah did survive and grew up. Fatimah married Ali PUH, her father's cousin, and had three children – Hasan, Husain and Zainab, peace upon them all. Today, their descendants are called Ahlul-Bayt – the people of the house (of the Prophet PBUH). **Allah** told the Prophet's family:

'And be regular in prayer, and give **zakah** and obey Allah and His Messenger. Allah only wants to remove from you all stain, O you members of the household, and to make you pure and spotless'. (**Qur'an** 33:33.)

> " My mum is from Ahlul-Bayt – the Prophet's family. She can trace her family back to the Prophet's grandson Husain PUH. She was born at Kerbala in Iraq, when her family travelled there to visit the tomb of Husain PUH. It's a responsibility to be from this family and I try to live up to it. "
> – *Husain*

Husain's mum shows him old photographs of her family and tells him all about them.

Help from Ahlul-Bayt means that these Iraqi children, in a refugee camp, are well fed and able to keep up with their schoolwork.

The Prophet's family life

Perhaps because his own sons died, the Prophet Muhammad PBUH especially loved his grandsons, Hasan PUH and Husain PUH. They looked a lot like their grandfather. He often carried them on his shoulders. Once, when he was speaking to people, the two little boys were toddling around and falling over. He cut short what he was saying, picked them up and sat them with him. He said to the people, 'Allah has spoken true – "...your possessions and your children are a trial..."' (Qur'an 8:28). (**Hadith**: Tirmidhi, Abu Dawud and Nisai in Mishkat ul-Masabih.)

After his farewell pilgrimage, the Prophet PBUH spoke to his followers at an oasis between **Makkah** and **Madinah**. Before the crowds went their separate ways, he told them that if they did not want to go wrong, they should follow the book of Allah – the Qur'an and 'the people of my house'. (Hadith: Muslim.)

The World Ahlul-Bayt Islamic League is a charity set up by the family of the Prophet PBUH. It provides education and helps people.

Ashura

This unit describes the martyrdom of Husain ibn Ali PUH.

> **Nobody likes bullies and nobody wants them to be in charge of things. The best people to be leaders are the ones who are fair to everyone. Muslims are taught to stick up for what is right and stand up to people who do bad things.**
> – *Fatimah*

On the 10th day of **Muharram**, the death of the grandson of the Prophet Muhammad PBUH is remembered.

Husain ibn Ali PUH

By the time the Prophet's grandson Husain PUH had children of his own, the numbers of **Muslims** had grown. Islam had spread very quickly. A man called Yazid had taken power in the Muslim world. He wanted everyone to accept him as 'Leader of the Believers'. Because he was powerful, lots of people accepted him as their leader. Husain PUH and his followers refused, because Yazid was not a good man. He was angry and made up his mind to force Husain PUH to accept him.

The dome and minarets of Imam Husain's tomb, Kerbala.

When they were travelling in the desert near Kerbala, Yazid's army stopped Husain PUH, his family and his followers from reaching the River Euphrates and getting water. They said that if Husain PUH would not accept Yazid they would kill him. Husain PUH told all the people with him to leave if they wanted to save their lives. None did as they were all loyal to him. In the battle that followed, Husain's group was greatly outnumbered. Lots of them were killed, including Husain PUH and many of his family. To make sure no-one else stood up to Yazid, the remaining family were sent to him in Damascus.

Traditions

Some Muslim children are taught to remember Husain PUH and to be thankful whenever they drink water. They learn to say this prayer:

'In the name of **Allah**, most Gracious, most Merciful. Blessings of Allah be upon **Imam** Husain, his family and his friends'.

In **Shi'ah** Muslim communities, people hold processions on Ashura. They act out the story of what happened in Kerbala and feel sad that anyone should treat the family of the Prophet PBUH so unjustly.

A modern leader of Iraq wanted everyone to bow to his leadership. When they would not, he attacked Kerbala and the tomb of Imam Husain PUH and killed many people.

Maulid

This unit tells you how Muslims celebrate the birthday of the Prophet Muhammad PBUH.

During the month of Rabi al-Awwal, the birthday of the Prophet Muhammad PBUH – the Maulid an-Nabi – is celebrated.

The Sunnah (tradition) of the Prophet PBUH

Copying the Prophet's example is called following the Sunnah – the customs of the Prophet Muhammad PBUH. The Prophet PBUH always got dressed from the right side first, so **Muslims** do the same. **Allah** tells people, 'You have indeed in the Messenger of Allah an excellent example'. (**Qur'an** 33:21.)

> " **My grandad tells me lots of stories about the Prophet Muhammad PBUH and how kind he was to people and to animals. The stories teach us that we should try to do what he did.** "
>
> – *Husain*

Husain's grandad can read and understand lots of languages so he translates the stories he knows for Husain.

Celebrating the Maulid

Many Muslims make this a time when they try to teach others about Islam. Muslim communities hold special events to celebrate the birthday of Prophet Muhammad PBUH. The Muslim Women's Association, which runs the only Muslim children's home in Britain, holds a Maulid Dinner every year. The members, their husbands, children and guests come to the function hall at a big mosque. The young people read **surahs** from the Qur'an and recite poems about the Prophet's life. A well-known person gives a short talk about Islam. Then everyone has an enjoyable meal and talks to their friends.

These Muslims from many different countries have gathered to read about the Prophet Muhammad's life.

The early life of the Prophet PBUH

Before the Prophet Muhammad PBUH was born in the city of **Makkah**, in the month of Rabi al-Awwal 570 CE, his father, Abdullah, had been taken ill and had died. His mother, Amina, asked her father-in-law to name her son. Muhammad, the name he chose, means 'Praised'. As a baby, Muhammad PBUH was sent out of the city to be cared for in the clean, desert air. He grew strong and healthy. At about 3 years old he went to Makkah to live with his mother. She died when he was 6. For 2 years he was lovingly cared for by his grandfather, until he too died. He then went to live with his uncle and became a favourite child in his big family.

Laylat-ul-Isra wal Mi'raj

This unit describes the night journey and ascension of Muhammad PBUH.

> **Every day, we offer our salah five times – before dawn, just after midday, in the afternoon, at sunset and at night-time. When we are at home, my family prays together. While everyone gets ready, I call the adhan in Arabic. Then my dad leads us in the prayer.**
> – *Husain*

This is the rock in Jerusalem from which the Prophet Muhammad PBUH ascended into the heavens. It is now protected by a beautiful golden domed building.

Many people try to spend the whole night in prayer, in remembrance of Muhammad's night journey and **mi'raj**, or ascent through the heavens.

'Glory to **Allah** who took His servant [Muhammad] for a journey by night from the Sacred Mosque [in Makkah] to the Farthest Mosque [in Jerusalem] whose surroundings We did bless.' (**Qur'an** 17:1.)

Pray 50 times a day!
One night, the Prophet Muhammad PBUH lay sleeping near the **Ka'bah** in **Makkah**. The angel **Jibril** woke him and took him to Jerusalem on the back of a white animal. There they met other prophets, including Ibrahim PUH, Musa PUH and Isa PUH. The Prophet Muhammad PBUH led them in prayer. The angel brought him two jugs. One jug was full of milk, the other was full of wine. Muhammad PBUH chose the milk and refused the wine. The angel said, 'You have made the right choice. Wine is forbidden for you and your people, the **Muslims**'.

The Prophet Muhammad PBUH was taken up through the seven heavens into the light of Allah's presence. He was told that Muslims should pray 50 times a day. The Prophet PBUH said that on his way back he met Musa PUH. He asked how many prayers Muhammad PBUH had been ordered to do. When he heard how many, Musa PUH said, 'Prayer is serious and people are weak. Go back and ask your Lord to make it less'. Muhammad PBUH did, and 10 prayers were taken off. The same thing happened several times again with Musa PUH, until only five prayers were left for the whole day. The Prophet PBUH said that he was ashamed to ask for less, and that whoever does the five prayers faithfully will have the reward for 50.

The map shows how far the Prophet Muhammad PBUH travelled from Makkah to Jerusalem and back again, on the night of his journey.

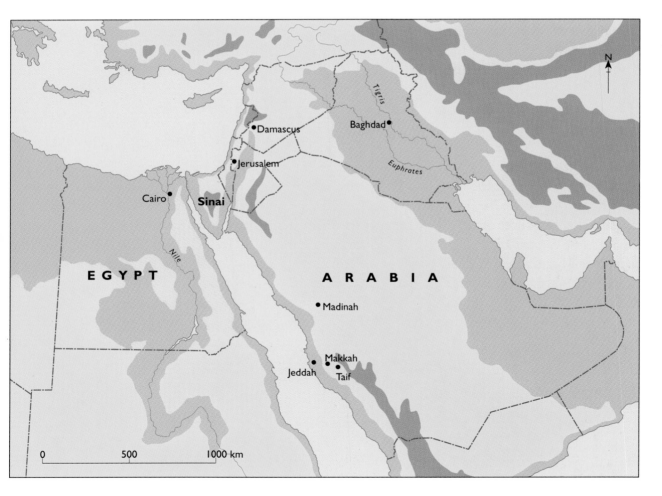

Laylat-ul-Barat

This unit is about the night of forgiveness.

Laylat-ul-Barat is the night of forgiveness, between the 14th and 15th days of the month of Shaban, when **Allah** decides each person's fate and provision for the coming year.

The night of forgiveness

Many **Muslims** believe that on Laylat-ul-Barat Allah decides what will happen to each person during the coming year. They believe Allah rewards their good actions and forgives them when they don't do everything they should. Many people stay up all night thanking Allah for their home, family and good things. They ask for His forgiveness when they are forgetful about Allah or anything in creation. They ask for Allah's blessings for everyone. Laylat-ul-Barat is 15 days before the start of the holy month of **Ramadan**. It is called 'the gateway to Ramadan'.

> " **When I see the good things Allah has given us, I want to thank Allah for fruit, flowers, vegetables, fish, animals and birds. Scientists are clever but no-one can make seeds to grow trees or crops. Allah created this world and everything in it so that we can eat, build homes and live well.**
> – *Husain* "

Husain is fascinated that even the bee, one of the smallest creatures, can make the beautifully patterned honeycomb.

This grand building in Jerusalem, with taps on two sides, supplies fresh drinking water for everyone.

Sharing

To show Allah how thankful they are for all the good things they have, Muslims give food to homeless people and to hostels. They also make long-term gifts that will do a lasting good.

'A man asked the Prophet PBUH, "Which charity is the most excellent?" He replied, "Water".' (**Hadith**: Abu Dawud.)

In hot, dusty countries, wealthy Muslims had wells dug and water fountains (Waqf fountains) built over them to provide free water for everyone. Many of these also had a drinking trough for animals. Some are still used, hundreds of years later. Other Muslims set up free schools, where anyone who was thirsty for knowledge could learn to read, write and study the **Qur'an**. Hospitals, too, were opened to give free treatment to all citizens. Farmers would set aside some trees from their orchards so that people could help themselves to the fruit or the fruit could be sold and the money given in charity.

Ramadan: the ninth month (1)

This unit tells you about fasting with the family.

When it's time to break fast, Husain really enjoys the taste of that first date.

" In Ramadan, we get up early, before it starts to get light. We have a meal. I like cornflakes and toast. We drink lots of tea and water. Before the first light of day we stop eating and say, 'I intend to fast today in obedience to Allah Most High'. "
– Husain

Muslims do not eat or drink from before dawn until sunset for the 29 or 30 days of the month of **Ramadan**. This fasting is called **sawm**.

'Ramadan is the month in which was sent down the **Qur'an**, as a guide to mankind…so every one of you who is present at their home during that month should spend it in fasting…' (Qur'an 2:185).

Fasting

For the first few days of Ramadan, fasting makes people feel a bit tired. When Ramadan is in the long days of summer, people often take a nap when they come home from school or work.

By sunset, everyone is ready to eat. After the **adhan**, the call to prayer, is made, people break their fast by eating a date and drinking. The Prophet PBUH said: 'When you break the fast, do so with dates. If you cannot find any dates, break the fast with water, because it is pure.' (**Hadith**: Mishkat al-Masabih.)

Fast FM:
keeping Muslims informed

In the north of England, a radio station called Fast FM broadcasts for 1 month every year. It has programmes of Qur'an reading and lets Muslims know the exact time for starting and breaking the fast each day. During Ramadan, many people stop listening to other radio stations and watching their usual TV programmes. They prefer to listen to Fast FM because it helps them concentrate on **Allah**.

A recipe for breaking the fast

Dates fried in butter and served with yoghurt

Ingredients
Dried or fresh dates
Butter
Plain yoghurt or fromage frais *or cream*

Method
Cut the dates in half. Remove the stones. Melt some butter in a small pan. Add the dates. Fry slowly for a few minutes until the dates have softened. Serve in individual dishes with the yoghurt or other topping.

Husain's family enjoys inviting people to break fast with them at home.

Ramadan: the ninth month (2)

This unit tells you about fasting with the community.

Fatimah likes to make sure her favourite foods are packed in the Ramadan basket her family takes to the mosque.

Caring for others

Every night during **Ramadan**, some large city mosques give an evening meal to hundreds of people. The food is sometimes served on trays like airline meals. The community tries to look after poor people, students, travellers and those who live alone or are separated from their families. They try to make sure that everyone who has fasted during the day has enough to eat. This food is paid for or given to the mosque by Muslims. In Cairo, 'Tables of Mercy' are set out in the street by kind people, so that the homeless may eat.

Ramadan in Muslim countries

In countries where most of the people are Muslim, schools don't need to have a lunch break during Ramadan. The pupils and teachers can go home much earlier. Lots of banks, businesses and offices close early to let the fasting workers go home to rest in the afternoon. During the day, most restaurants and cafés are closed until after sunset. In the evening lots of shops are open because people like to do some shopping at night on their way to and from the mosque.

How long is the fast?

Because the Islamic calendar moves back through the seasons by about 11 days per year (see pages 6–7), no-one always has to fast in the hottest season of the year, or on the longest summer days. In Britain in mid-summer, people can be fasting during the daylight hours from about 2.35am till 9.20pm, which is almost 19 hours. In the year 2,000, when Ramadan falls in December, Muslims will fast from about 6.15am until 4pm, which is fewer than 10 hours without food or drink.

These Palestinian women are happy to spend every day during Ramadan preparing food for their community to break fast together each night.

29

Laylat-ul-Qadr

This unit is about the night of power.

When he was alone in a cave on this mountain, the Prophet Muhammad PBUH learned the first words of Allah's revealed Qu'ran.

The first revelation of the **Qur'an** came to the Prophet PBUH on **Laylat-ul-Qadr** – the night of power. It is a blessed night – one of the last 10 nights of **Ramadan** – and **Muslims** try to spend it in prayer.

"**When you get a new video or computer game you read the instructions carefully to find out everything it can do, so that you can play it well. Muslims read the Qur'an to find out Allah's instructions about how to live a good life. Allah created us so He understands what we need to know and do to be happy and successful.**"

– Husain

The first revelation

Makkah was a busy, noisy city. The Prophet Muhammad PBUH liked to go to the desert to enjoy the peace. One night, while he was there, the angel Jibril spoke to him. 'Recite,' said **Jibril**. Muhammad PBUH was too afraid to speak. Three times the angel repeated the words, 'Recite, in the name of your Lord who has created, created man out of a germ cell. Recite! And your Lord is the Most Bountiful'. (Qur'an 96:1–3.)

Muhammad PBUH said the words back to the angel. He had learned the first words of **Allah**'s revealed Qur'an. For the next 23 years, he learned more and taught it to others.

The town is brightly lit to attract and welcome everyone on this special night.

The night of power in Morocco

In Morocco, Laylat-ul-Qadr is a wonderful night. Towns are brilliantly lit with thousands of light bulbs strung around the mosques and across the narrow streets. To celebrate, people try to pray in as many mosques as they can between the night and early morning **salah**. Groups of friends walk from mosque to mosque, praying in each place. On the way, they meet other friends and sometimes join up with new groups. The whole town seems to be happily, noisily on the move. Once inside the mosque, the atmosphere is quiet, peaceful and devoted to prayer and the love of Allah.

Id-ul-Fitr

This unit describes the festival of breaking the fast.

On Id day, Fatimah doesn't go to school and after going to the mosque, celebrates with her family and friends.

> **The month of Ramadan is over on the morning after the new moon has been sighted. That is the day of Id-ul-Fitr, the first of the month of Shawal. In our house we get up early ready to go to the mosque. We're lucky because we've got two bathrooms, so everyone can have their shower in time and put on fresh clothes. Our family likes to arrive at the mosque early so that we can find a space inside. People who come later have to pray in the courtyard.**
>
> *– Fatimah*

The Prophet Muhammad PBUH said, 'Do not begin the month of fasting until you have seen the crescent of the new moon, and do not finish the month of fasting until you have seen the next new moon. If it is covered with clouds, when you think it should be visible, add an extra day of fasting'. (**Hadith**: Bukhari.)

Zakat-ul-Fitr

All adult **Muslims**, men and women, who are the heads of households, have to pay **zakat-ul-Fitr** for themselves and everyone they look after in their family. The amount for each person is the price of a meal. So that every Muslim, however poor, can join in the **Id** day feast, zakat-ul-Fitr ought to be paid before **Id-ul-Fitr**. It can be given directly to the people in need, or it can be given to the mosque **zakah** committee, who will give it out for the community.

On Id, when people arrive at the mosque, they join in reciting the Id **Takbirs**. They are in Arabic and begin with the words '**Allahu Akbar**'.

The Id Takbirs

Allah is great, Allah is great,
Allah is great,
There is no god except Allah,
Allah is great, Allah is great,
To Him belongs all praise,
Allah is the greatest,
All praise is due to Him,
And glory to Allah,
In the evening and the morning,
There is no god except Allah the Unique.

On Id days the mosques are filled to overflowing and many people make their salah in the outside courtyards.

Sadaqah, zakah, khums

This unit explains how Muslims give for the sake of Allah.

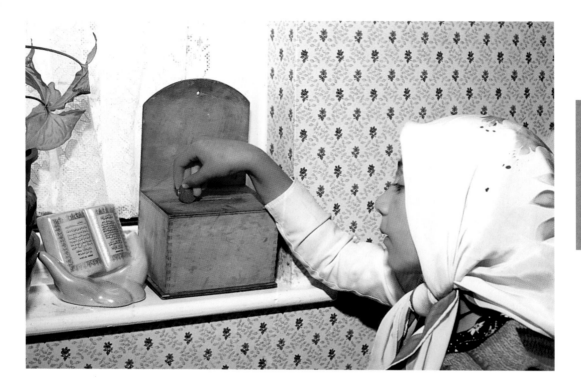

It is good to try to fill the sadaqah box quickly because there are people all over the world who need help.

" **At home, we keep a charity box for our gifts of sadaqah – charity, near the front door. Before we go out, the family puts some money into it. Even if we only put in a few pence, the box soon fills up. We use the money to give to charities.** "

– Fatimah

The Prophet Muhammad PBUH and charity

The Prophet Muhammad PBUH was praying in his mosque in **Madinah**. His friends were surprised that as soon as he finished, he walked quickly to his house. Some followed him to ask why he had hurried off. He answered, 'I remembered I had some money and wanted to give it to the poor'. (**Hadith**: Bukhari.)

Zakah – collecting and giving

Zakah is welfare tax and the way the **Muslim** communities make sure that those who can afford it help those in need. Every year, **Sunni** Muslims give away two and a half per cent of whatever money, goods and property they have after they have paid all their own bills. People can pay the money directly to those in need, or to a zakah committee at their mosque. If Muslims know about someone who is too shy to ask for help, they will tell the zakah committee about them.

Khums – paid to help the community

Shi'ah Muslims pay zakah on nine kinds of wealth. They also pay **khums** – one fifth of what is left after they have paid their bills.

'And know that whatever thing you gain, a fifth of it is for Allah, and for the Messenger and for the near of kin and the orphans and the needy and the wayfarer...' (**Qur'an** 8:41).

Islamic aid agencies

The Red Crescent is an international Islamic aid agency. It works in war zones and countries which have faced disasters. Muslim Aid and Islamic Relief also help suffering people, whoever and wherever they are. Islamic Relief began with a gift of 20p. Now their volunteers help 4,000 orphans in over 10 countries. Interpal supports widows and orphans in Palestine. Each of them depends on the zakah and **sadaqah** donations of Muslims world-wide.

Islamic aid agencies send out leaflets to tell people how they can help charities to continue to help others.

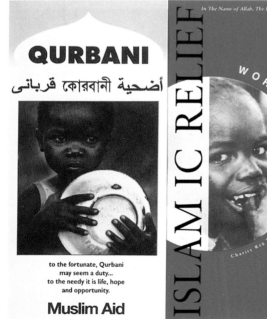

Hajj

This unit tells you why the pilgrimage to Makkah and other places in Arabia is one of the main duties of Muslims.

> **My dad told us that he had saved up enough for us to go on Hajj. I could hardly believe that I would see the Ka'bah and the places where the Prophet PBUH had lived. It would be the journey of a lifetime.**
> – *Husain*

The Ka'bah is a very old building. Muslims believe it was the first house made for the worship of the One True God. The word Ka'bah means 'cube-shaped'.

What is Hajj?

Hajj takes place during set days in the month of **Dhul-Hijjah**. Every **Muslim** who is healthy and can afford the cost must make the pilgrimage at least once in his or her life. Muslims look forward to completing Hajj. Pilgrims remember that the **Ka'bah** is the first house built for the worship of the One True God. It was built by the Prophet Ibrahim PUH and his son Ismail PUH over 4,000 years ago. Pilgrims also remember that the Prophet Muhammad PBUH once helped when the Ka'bah was being repaired. Pilgrims walk around the Ka'bah seven times, praying to **Allah**.

Crowds of pilgrims gather at Arafat where the Prophet Muhammad PBUH gave his last speech.

Ismail's mother, Hajar, searched for water for her baby son by hurrying between two hills, and pilgrims follow in her footsteps. Then, at the plain of Arafat, pilgrims think about what the Prophet PBUH said in his last speech and ask Allah for His forgiveness. Pilgrims then throw stones at three pillars at **Mina** in memory of Ismail PUH, who threw stones at the devils who wanted him to disobey his father Ibrahim PUH.

'Then when you pour down from Arafat, remember Allah at the holy place and celebrate His praises.' (**Qur'an** 2:198.)

Teaching Muslims how to live

The millions of Muslims who go each year to Hajj are of every colour and from every country on earth. Each person is a part of the world-wide community of Muslims. Being together on Hajj teaches them about loving their neighbour. Travelling together is a lesson for everyone in being kind and patient.

A Hajj diary

This unit describes Husain's diary of the pilgrimage.

Husain made all his preparations and put on his pilgrim clothes, 'Ihram', before setting off on Hajj.

> **My whole family came to see us off. At the check-in, big Hajj stickers were put on our luggage. Everyone on our plane seemed to be a Muslim on the way to Hajj. I took a notebook and wrote down everything we did.**
>
> *– Husain*

Arriving in Arabia

Our flight to Jeddah lasted 6 hours. Planes were arriving from all over the world. We saw **Muslims** from Indonesia, Senegal and the USA. People were speaking in lots of different languages, but everyone greeted us in Arabic, saying 'peace be with you'. It was as if we all knew one another. Everyone got on buses and set off for **Makkah**. It was very hot.

Changing into Ihram

Ten miles away from Makkah, the bus stopped and everyone who had not yet prepared themselves for **Ihram**, the state of purity and readiness for **Hajj**, got out. They showered and changed into pilgrim clothes. All the men were dressed in two large white cloths. Many of the women wore white dresses and headscarves.

Entering Makkah and seeing the Ka'bah

I'll never forget seeing the **Ka'bah** for the first time. I didn't know it would be so big, yet it looked as though it could rise up out of the huge crowds. We thanked **Allah** for blessing us with this visit to His house. Then we walked around the Ka'bah. It took a long time and it seemed as though everyone in the world was there with us. Then we sat in the mosque and drank **Zamzam** water, which Allah had provided for Ismail PUH and Hajar and all the pilgrims for thousands of years up to today.

Every year during the Hajj, more than 2 million Muslims from all over the world gather to pray by the Ka'bah.

Mina and Arafat

On the days of Hajj, all the pilgrims went out of Makkah to **Mina** and Arafat, where we prayed for ourselves, our family and friends. The next day was **Id**. We stoned the pillars and visited the Ka'bah. Everyone was very tired. The time for Ihram was over and we spent the next 2 days at Mina. I made friends with a German boy called Hasan. My mum said we made a good pair – 'Hasan and Husain', like the grandsons of the Prophet PBUH.

Id-ul-Adha

This unit tells you about the festival of the sacrifice.

Muslims sacrifice a sheep or a goat on the 10th day of **Dhul-Hijjah** to commemorate what happened to the Prophet Ibrahim PUH and his son Ismail PUH, and how they were willing to obey **Allah**.

Pilgrims often bring home Zamzam water from Makkah, to share its blessings with family and friends.

> **Last year my uncle and his family went to Hajj. They brought back Zamzam water for us. I asked them lots of questions about Hajj. My auntie liked being near the Ka'bah. My cousins liked sleeping in the big tents at Mina and my uncle said everything about Hajj made him want to go again.**
> – *Fatimah*

What happens on Id-ul-Adha

Early in the morning of **Id-ul-Adha**, Muslims shower and put on their best clean clothes. They set off to the largest mosque in their area. The Id prayer is an extra prayer between early morning and midday. The **Imam** leads the people in prayer. Then he talks about the meaning and importance of **Id**. He often reminds everyone about the sense of community among people on **Hajj**. He encourages Muslims to keep this feeling for the whole year.

Many Islamic relief agencies give meat to Muslims in need all over the world, so that they can all join in the feast which is held on Id-ul-Adha.

The Prophet Ibrahim PUH and his son Ismail PUH

Ibrahim PUH was an old man when he prayed, 'O my Lord! Grant me a righteous son!'. Allah answered his prayer and his son Ismail PUH was born. When he grew up and was old enough to work alongside his father, Ibrahim PUH dreamt that he should sacrifice his son. He told Ismail PUH and asked him what he thought. His son answered, 'O my father, do as you are commanded. You will find me, if Allah so wills, one of the steadfast'. They were both willing to obey what they thought Allah wanted and got ready to sacrifice Ismail PUH. But Allah spoke to them, saying, 'O Ibrahim, you have already fulfilled the purpose of the dream'. Because they had been so obedient, Allah gave them a sheep to sacrifice instead. (Qur'anic quotes taken from 37:100–105.)

On Id day these Muslims have come to the mosque to hear their Imam, Sheikh Nazim, teach about respect for all of Allah's creation.

Jumu'ah

This unit is about the weekly Friday congregational prayer.

It's time for prayer and Husain is calling the adhan to let everyone know. 'Come to prayer; come to success.'

Coming together

Every Friday, local **Muslims** come together for **Jumu'ah**. Twice a year, Muslim communities gather for **Id**, and once in each Muslim's life he or she has the chance on **Hajj** to be with Muslims from all over the world.

66 **Every Friday I go with my family to Salat-ul-Jumu'ah – the Friday prayer at the main mosque in our town. I look forward to it because I know I will meet all my friends after the prayer. At our mosque, there is a room for babies and small children to play, so that they don't disturb the people who want to listen and pray.** 99

– Husain

On Friday, people leave work in time to get to the mosque.

'O you who believe! When the call to prayer is proclaimed on Friday (the day of assembly) hasten earnestly to the remembrance of **Allah** and leave off business…And when the prayer is finished, then may you disperse throughout the land and seek the bounty of Allah: and remember Allah frequently, that you may prosper.' (**Qur'an** 62:9–10.)

Jumu'ah salah

Because Friday is the day that Muslims meet together and pray, it is the community's weekly celebration. On Friday, after their shower, people put on fresh clothes to go to the mosque. However, it is not a holiday. In the morning, up to midday, most people are at work or school as usual. During their lunch break, they go to the mosque. Part of the Salat-ul-Jumu'ah is to listen to the talk by the **Imam**. He tells the people important things about Islamic events and gives them advice about everyday life. The Imam tries to make his talk interesting to young people and adults.

The mosque

There are more than 500 mosques in Britain. Most universities and even some hospitals have a place where the Muslims who work and study can come together to perform Salat-ul-Jumu'ah. Muslims in Europe save up to build mosques big enough to hold all of their community for festivals and Friday prayers. A mosque can be a real community centre for people.

Glossary

Adhan call to prayer. A Mu'adhin is the person who makes the call to prayer.

al-Kafi the title of the books of Hadith, put together by Muhammad ibn-Yaqub Kolieni, a Shi'ah scholar.

Allah the Islamic name for the One True God in the Arabic language.

Allahu Akbar 'Allah is Most Great'.

Dhul-Hijjah the month of the Hajj, the last month of the Islamic year.

fajr (Salat-ul-Fajr) the dawn salah, which may be performed from dawn until just before sunrise.

hadith the sayings of the Prophet Muhammad PBUH, as reported by his friends, children and household. These are an important source of Islamic law.

Hajj the annual pilgrimage to Makkah, which each Muslim must undertake at least once in a lifetime, if he or she has the health and wealth.

Hijrah 'departure'. The emigration, or departure, of the Prophet Muhammad PBUH from Makkah to Madinah in 622 CE. The Islamic calendar starts with this event.

Id 'happiness'; a religious holiday, a feast to thank Allah and celebrate a happy occasion.

Id-ul-Adha celebration of the sacrifice, to remember how obedient the Prophets Ibrahim and Isma'il (peace be upon them) were to Allah.

Id-ul-Fitr celebration of breaking the fast on the day after Ramadan ends, which is also the first day of Shawal, the 10th Islamic month.

Ihram the state that Muslims must be in to perform Hajj. Also the name of the two plain, white, unsewn cloths worn by male pilgrims to show the equality and purity of pilgrims.

Imam 'leader'; a man who leads Muslims together in prayer.

Jibril Gabriel the angel, who delivered Allah's messages to His Prophets.

jumu'ah (Salat-ul-Jumu'ah) the weekly community salah and talk, shortly after midday on Fridays.

Ka'bah a cube-shaped building in the centre of the grand mosque in Makkah; the first house built for the worship of Allah, the One True God.

khums a contribution made by Shi'ah Muslims of one-fifth of their extra income every year.

Laylat-ul-Qadr the night of power, when the first revelation of the Qur'an was made to Prophet Muhammad PBUH.

Madinah 'city', the City of the Prophet, the name given to the place where Muhammad PBUH went to live.

Makkah the city where Prophet Muhammad PBUH was born and where the Ka'bah is located.

Mina the place near Makkah where pilgrims stay on the 10th, 11th and 12th of Duhl-Hijjah and perform some of the activities of the Hajj.

mi'raj the ascent through the heavens of Prophet Muhammad PBUH.

Muharram the first month in the Islamic calendar, which is calculated from the time the Prophet PBUH moved to Madinah.

Muslim someone who claims to have accepted Islam by saying the shahadah.

PBUH 'peace and blessings of Allah upon him'; the words said in Arabic by Muslims every time the Prophet Muhammad PBUH is mentioned.

PUH 'peace be upon him'; the words said in Arabic by Muslims every time prophets and the twelve Shi'ah Imams are mentioned.

Qur'an the Divine Book, revealed to Prophet Muhammad PBUH. Allah's final revelation to mankind.

Ramadan the ninth month of the Islamic calendar, when Muslims fast from just before dawn until sunset, as ordered by Allah in the Qur'an.

sadaqah a voluntary payment or good action for charity.

salah communication with and worship of Allah, taught by the Prophet Muhammad PBUH and recited in the Arabic language. The five daily times of salah are fixed by Allah.

sawm fasting from just before dawn until sunset; not eating any food or drink (including water).

shahadah a declaration of faith: 'There is no god except Allah, Muhammad is the Messenger of Allah.'

Shi'ah 'followers' – Muslims who believe that Ali PUH should have been the successor of the Prophet Muhammad PBUH.

Sunni Muslims who accept that Abu Bakr, Umar, Uthman and Ali (may Allah be pleased with them) were the rightful leaders of the Muslims after the Prophet Muhammad PBUH.

surah a division of the Qur'an (there are 114 in all).

Takbir saying 'Allahu Akbar!' during Salah, Id and other occasions.

zakah every year Muslims have to pay a set proportion of their wealth to help others.

zakat-ul-Fitr paying money for the benefit of others at the end of Ramadan.

Zamzam the well near the Ka'bah in Makkah, where water first sprang in answer to Hajar's search and prayers.

Further reading

World Religions: Islam. Khadijah Knight; Wayland (Publishers) Ltd, 1995.

Religions through Festivals: Islam. Alan Brine, ed. Clive Erricker; Longman, 1989.

Discovering Religions: Islam. Sue Penney; Heinemann Publishers (Oxford) Ltd, 1995.

Discovering Sacred Texts: The Qur'an. Ruqaiyyah Waris Maqsood, ed. W. Owen Cole; Heinemann Publishers (Oxford) Ltd, 1994.

Understanding Religions: Food and Fasting. Deidre Burke, Wayland (Publishers) Ltd, 1992.

Understanding Religions: Pilgrimages and Journeys. Katherine Prior, Wayland (Publishers) Ltd, 1992.

A closer look

This picture shows pilgrims gathering at Arafat, where the Prophet Muhammad PBUH gave his last speech. In this speech he told Muslims that whatever their race or colour, everyone is equal before Allah. Each one of them should be trustworthy and responsible for their own actions. They should not oppress people or charge interest on any loan. Women should be treated fairly. He reminded them of their duties as Muslims – five times salah daily, fast in Ramadan, complete their Hajj, pay Zakah and believe in the one true God. He asked if he had been clearly understood and the people answered 'Yes'.

Index

Plain numbers (3) refer to the text. Italic numbers (*3*) refer to a picture.

adhan 22, 27
Ahlul-Bayt 16-17
aid agencies 35, *35*, 40
alcohol 22
Allah 4, 5, 6, 8, 12, 16, 20, 23, 24, 30, 31, 37, 39, 41
Arabic language 8
Arafat *36*, 37, 39
Ashura 18-19

beliefs, Muslim 4, 5, 8, 24

Cairo 28
calendar, lunar 6, 14, 29
Cave Hira *30*
charity 17, *17*, 25, 28, 33, 34-5, *34*
communal eating 28, *28*, 29, *29*
congregational prayer, weekly 42-3

Day of Judgement 5
Dome of the Rock *22*

fajr (Salat-ul-Fajr) 7
Fast FM radio 27
fasting 5, 26-9
    breaking the fast *26*, 27, 32-3

hadith 10-11, *11*, 17, 25, 27, 32, 34
Hajj 5, 36-9, *37*, 40, 42
Hijrah 14-15
Hijrah calendar 6, *7*
Husain Ibn Ali 16, 17, 18-19

Ibrahim 37, 40, 41
Id 33, 39, 40, 42
Id prayer 40
Id-ul-Adha 40-1
Id-ul-Fitr 32-3

Ihram 38
Imam 40, 43
Interpal 35
Islamic Relief 35
Ismail 37, 39, 40, 41

Jabal-ur-Rahma *36*
Jerusalem 22, *23*
Jibril 22, 31
jumu'ah (Salat-ul-Jumu'ah) 42-3

Ka'bah 5, 37, 39, *39*, 40
Kerbala 13, 16, *18*, 19, *19*
khums 35

law, Islamic 10
Laylat-ul-Barat 24
Laylat-ul-Isra wal Mi'raj 22-3
Laylat-ul-Qadr 30-1, *31*

Madinah 9, 14, 15, *15*, 34, 36
madrassa (Qur'anic school) 9
Makkah 13, 14, 21, 22, *23*, 31, 36, 38, 39
Maulid an-Nabi 20-1, *21*
Mina 37, 39, 40
Morocco 31
mosques 29, 31, 32, 33, *33*, 40, 42, *42*, 43, *43*
Muhammad, Prophet 4, 5, 6, 8, 9, 37
    birthday 20-1
    early life 21
    migration to Madinah 14-15
    night journey and ascension 22-3
    Prophet's family 16-17
    revelation of the Qur'an 30, 31
    sayings (hadith) 10-11, *11*, 17, 25, 27, 32, 34
Musa 22, 23
Muslim Aid 35
Muslim Women's Association 21

night journey 22-3
night of forgiveness 24
night of power 30-1

pilgrimage *see* Hajj
prayer mats 13
prayer and worship *see* salah
principles of Islam 4, 5

Qur'an 4, 5, 6, 8-9, *8*, 10, 12, 16, 17, 20, 26, 27, 30, 31, 35, 37, 41, 43
    surahs (sections) 8, 21

Ramadan 5, 24, 26-9, 30, 32
Red Crescent 35

sacrifice 40, 41
sadaqah 34, *34*, 35
salah 5, 7, 12-13, *13*, 22, 23, 31, 40, 42-3
sawm 5, 26-9, 32
shahadah 5
Shi'ah Muslims 5, 13, 19, 35
sun and times of prayer 7
Sunnah (tradition) of the Prophet 20
Sunni Muslims 5, 35

Takbirs 33
Tala'al badru alaynaa 15
teaching, Islamic 5, 10
    see also hadith

Waqf fountains 25, *25*
way of life, Islamic 5, 37
welfare tax *see* zakah
World Ahlul-Bayt Islamic League 17, *17*

Yazid 18, 19

zakah 5, 16, 33, 35
zakat-ul-Fitr 33
Zamzam water 39, *40*
Zayd Ibn Thabit 9